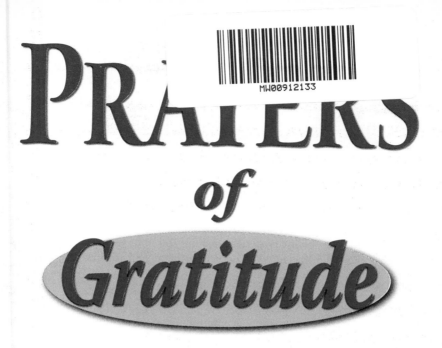

PRAYERS

of

Gratitude

Contributing Writers

Nancy Parker Brummett

Lain Ehmann

Marie D. Jones

Publications International, Ltd.

Cover Photo: Shutterstock

Contributing Writers

Nancy Parker Brummett is a freelance writer, columnist, and the author of four books who lives in Colorado Springs, CO. Leading women closer to the heart of God is the hallmark of her speaking and writing ministries. To learn more about her life and work, visit www.nancyparkerbrummett.com.

Lain Ehmann is a Massachusetts-based writer and mom to three.

Marie D. Jones is the author of several best-selling nonfiction books and a contributing author to numerous inspirational books, including *Echoes of Love: Sisters, Mother, Grandmother, Friends, Graduation, Wedding; Mother's Daily Prayer Book;* and *When You Lose Someone You Love: God Will Comfort You.* She can be reached at www.mariedjones.com.

Acknowledgments

Scripture quotations are taken from the *New Revised Standard Version* of the Bible. Copyright © 1989 by the Division of Christian Education of the National Council of the Churches of Christ in the United States of America. Used by permission. All rights reserved.

Louis Weber, CEO
Publications International, Ltd.
7373 North Cicero Avenue
Lincolnwood, Illinois 60712

ISBN-13: 978-1-4508-0144-7
ISBN-10: 1-4508-0144-7

Manufactured in USA.

8 7 6 5 4 3 2 1

GRATITUDE TO GOD

When we are grateful for what we have, God gives us even more. For the blessings of a grateful heart are many, and the prayers of a grateful heart are answered in kind. Too often, our focus is on the things we lack, have lost, or dream of having one day, not on the wonderful things we are already surrounded with. Prayers of gratitude help us shift our focus from what we lack to love and thankfulness. And when we do, we suddenly begin to see things we never noticed before, blessings big and small that have always been there in our lives, just awaiting our attention.

Just as we turn to God for prayers of supplication and in times of fear and weakness, we should also turn to God in celebration, in thanks, and in happiness for all we have received. Even God likes to receive good news, and our prayers of positivity make the angels sing with joy.

We don't just have to thank God for what we have, we can also thank him for what others have. Gratitude can reach beyond our own hearts and souls to touch those we love, for as we give thanks for the joy and happiness of others, we often find joy and happiness expanding in our own lives as well. This is the promise of God, he will give to those who have faith in his love—and who live in a state of thankfulness—a heart that is ready to receive even more.

Prayers of Gratitude

God, how can I ever thank you enough for the blessings in my life? Each time I turn around, I see something to be grateful for, some small miracle that makes my heart sing and reminds me that you are always present and always working for my highest good. I thank you for the daily joys that greet me when I rise each morning and for the calm and peace that is in my heart knowing that I am always being loved, watched over, and cared for. Thank you, God.

Truly I tell you, this poor widow has put in more than all those who are contributing to the treasury. For all of them have contributed out of their abundance; but she out of her poverty has put in everything she had, all she had to live on.
—Mark 12:43–44

4

Prayers of Gratitude

Father, you say that to those who have faith, more shall be given, and for me that has always been true. I have not always been strong in my faith, and during those times I have felt dragged down by circumstances. But as I turn my heart back in your direction, I begin once again to see how I am constantly and eternally blessed and how my faith is what brings your good into my life. Without faith, I have nothing. With faith, my faith in you, I have everything I could ever want and more. Amen.

Lord Jesus, when I contemplate the enormity of your sacrifice for me, I can barely contain my thankfulness. There are no words to describe what you gave our fallen world. I am undeserving, yet I fully accept your gifts with arms and heart wide open. I ask that you help me make my life a living testament to your love. Amen.

Lord, how inadequate for us to set aside one day in the year on which we are officially thankful! Every breath we take, every task we undertake, every life we touch—every part of every day we live should be offered up to you in thanksgiving! So, Lord, this year let me truly enter into your gates with thanksgiving, but don't let me stop there. Instead, I want to also enthusiastically enter into your courts with praise! For it is in praising you for who you are that we express the most gratitude of all.

Enter his gates with thanksgiving, and his courts with praise. Give thanks to him, bless his name.
—Psalm 100:4

Lord, everything around me is a miracle and a gift from you. Each blade of grass, the laugh of a baby, the wind in the trees . . . they are all

created by you. Even the challenges I come
across are lessons for me, to help me grow
in spirit and become more Christlike in my
thoughts and actions. Thank you for every
experience, because when I approach each relationship and opportunity with your guidance,
I move further along my journey toward you. I
thank you, Amen.

Lord, today as I look around me, my heart is
full of gratitude for all the blessings of an ordinary day. I don't take for granted the fact that I
have a roof over my head and plenty of food to
serve my family. I appreciate the ability to sim-
ply fall into the routine of a busy day with no
major disasters, crises, or life-changing experiences. The ordinary day is a precious gift, Lord,
and I'm so glad I know whom to thank for it.

Lord, I sat down with a big list of things to ask you for. Material needs and wants, people to reach, hearts to change, and situations where your presence is needed. But as I began to pray, I realized how many blessings I already have in my life and that I have more than I could ever need. So I am setting aside my list of petitions, and I want to say only this: Thank you. Thank you for being a loving and responsive God who anticipates and answers my needs. Amen.

Every generous act of giving, with every perfect gift, is from above, coming down from the Father of lights, with whom there is no variation or shadow due to change.
—James 1:17

God, I know that lately all I have been doing is praying and asking for things, complaining

about what I don't have and experiencing the
sadness of what I have lost. Please don't think
I'm not grateful for your presence in my life. I
am grateful. It's just that sometimes life challenges my gratitude, and I have to come back to
you and talk with you to get quiet in my heart
and mind so I can remember that I already
have all I need . . . in you. Amen.

Happy is the one who listens to me,
watching daily at my gates,
waiting beside my doors.
For whoever finds me finds life
and obtains favor from the Lord.
—Proverbs 8:34–35

Lord, I want to go through my day energized
by thankfulness! Help me deal with unpleasant
people from the generosity of gratitude, not the

scarcity of selfishness. Remind me that short-falls can be windfalls when I learn to be appreciative of what I have, not focused on what I don't have. Seal this attitude of gratitude in my heart, Lord, that I may draw others closer to you. Make me a reflection of your glory—a person with a grateful heart.

This is the day that the Lord has made;
let us rejoice and be glad in it.
—Psalm 118:24

Today, Lord, I want to be guided by a grateful heart. As I understand it, a grateful heart doesn't search for what's missing but delights in what's present. A grateful heart expects the best from others and gives its best in return. A grateful heart forgets what might have been and enjoys every moment of each new day as it

comes. A grateful heart is a prayer of its own—
one that fills the heavens with praise! Please,
Lord, give me a grateful heart.

━━ ━━

Heavenly Father, I thank you for the abundance of blessings you continue to bring into
my life. I appreciate my family and friends, the
walls around me, the clothing I wear, and the
food I eat. Each and every one of these comes
only through your love and continued devotion
to me. All that I am, all that I have, all that I
will be is because of you. Amen.

━━ ━━

Father in Heaven, you tell us that whatever we
ask for, you will give us. Lately, though, I feel
like you haven't heard my prayers. I believe you
are faithful and loving, wanting only the best
for me. So I come to you in prayer to ask again,
and to thank you, for I am certain in time you

will answer my prayers in ways I cannot even imagine. Thank you for being a loving God, allowing me to petition you for all my heart's desires. Amen.

❧ ❧

Ask, and it will be given you;
search, and you will find;
knock, and the door will be opened for you.
For everyone who asks receives,
and everyone who searches finds,
and for everyone who knocks,
the door will be opened.
—Matthew 7:7–8

❧ ❧

Lord, I need to confess something today. In spite of all the riches you've given me, I sometimes find myself wanting something someone else has—that perfect job, a larger house, or even those great-looking shoes! Forgive me for being so ungrateful, Lord. You have blessed me in so many ways. You have given me riches beyond compare through your Son, Jesus Christ! Please decrease my greed, Lord, and increase my gratitude. Amen.

It is good to give thanks to the Lord.
—Psalm 92:1

There she is, Lord, that little cat that you brought into my life—one of your most endearing creatures for sure. How relaxing it is to stroke her soft fur as she curls up in my lap. How much I can learn from her about making time to play—and about finding the sunniest spots in life! You have blessed us with pets to make our hearts glad and to be our companions through the sunshine and the rain. We don't want to forget to thank you, Lord, for them.

We're so glad you took the time to create them, for they make our lives so much richer.

Each day brings new things to be happy about, God, and I am really loving my life for the first time in a long time. I am so grateful for this new way of looking at things, seeing the glass half full instead of half empty and always looking on the bright side. Your blessings are everywhere, but it took me awhile to notice them because I was so caught up in the stress and strain of my daily life. Thank you for opening my eyes to a whole new world of wonder and joy.

God, thank you for the ability to serve others and fulfill their needs. Whether I'm lending a hand, sharing a kind word, or providing a meal, when I help another person and see gratitude in their eyes, I know I am doing your work here on earth. Please help me recognize all the opportunities I have to serve so that I can give back a small fraction of the many blessings you have given me.

And the king will answer them,
"Truly I tell you, just as you did it to one
of the least of these who are members
of my family, you did it to me."
—Matthew 25:40

Heavenly Father, thank you for being there when I needed you today. I was scared and confused, and I turned to you in prayer and asked for your guidance. You were immediately with me, surrounding me with your presence. The challenges I was facing didn't go away, but I was able to see them more clearly and realize they are less significant than I had feared. I am so grateful that you are always with me, always ready to help me in my times of need. Thank you for your love for me. Amen.

⇒ ⇐

*Be strong and bold; have no fear or dread of them,
because it is the Lord your God who goes with you;
he will not fail you or forsake you.*
—Deuteronomy 31:6

⇒ ⇐

Almighty God, while I often thank you for your provision and your intervention, I'm afraid I don't thank you often enough for all the unseen ways you work in my life. Was there a temptation you led me away from this week? Did you steer me in a different direction so I would avoid the traffic accident I heard about on the evening news? Did you help me make a smarter choice in some area of my life? In this moment I want to thank you for the many blessings that may have come my way that only you know. And I will continue to thank you as long as I live.

✦✦

O Lord, you have searched me and known me.
You know when I sit down and when I rise up;
you discern my thoughts from far away.
You search out my path and my lying down,
and are acquainted with all my ways.
Even before a word is on my tongue,
O Lord, you know it completely.
You hem me in, behind and before,
and lay your hand upon me.
Such knowledge is too wonderful for me;
it is so high that I cannot attain it.
—Psalm 139:1–6

✦✦

God, my heart sings out today for all the good I have received. You have graced me with the love of so many wonderful people and prospered me in truly amazing ways. Each day I find new reasons to be grateful. Some are big, some are small, but all these things make me feel loved and cherished by you. Thank you for giving me a life that is truly fulfilling and for surrounding me with miracles big and small. Amen.

*And now I am about to go the way of all the earth,
and you know in your hearts and souls,
all of you, that not one thing has failed of all the
good things that the Lord your God promised
concerning you; all have come to pass for you,
not one of them has failed.*
—Joshua 23:14

Lord, so many people are blind to the miracles of the world around us. They go through life without noticing or experiencing your gifts. They miss the beauty of the natural world, they miss the miracle of love, and they miss the very joy of being alive. Please help me recognize these blessings and also let me help others realize that every second of life is to be cherished and appreciated. Amen.

O Lord my God, I will give thanks to you forever.
—Psalm 30:12

Lord, because you know me well, you know that there was a time in my life when I was so busy and moving so fast that I didn't notice the birds. How sad is that? I am so grateful to you for slowing me down, Lord. Now when I see birds at my feeder, along with all the other

wonders of your miraculous creation, my heart
overflows with thanksgiving. I wouldn't have
wanted to miss this glorious world of yours,
Lord! Thank you for getting my attention.

*A new heart I will give you,
and a new spirit I will put within you;
and I will remove from your body the heart of
stone and give you a heart of flesh.*
—Ezekiel 36:26

Lord, please help me be more focused on the
good in life and less focused on the bad. I know
that faith is what brings good things into my
world, but sometimes my faith gets a little
shaky and I end up dwelling on the bad stuff
going on around me. Show me how to open
my heart back up and see things with new eyes.
Change my perspective so that I can under-

stand on a deeper level that what is happening to me is a blessing and not a curse. For this I am grateful, Lord.

≫ ≪

Lord, thank you for sending Jesus Christ to show us how to live. Through his life, death, and rebirth, you demonstrated not only the depths of your dedication to us, but you also provided a concrete example to the world of how to live as a complete expression of love. Thank you for giving us your most beloved, your one and only Son, so that we, too, can have eternal life. Amen.

≫ ≪

Thank you, thank you, thank you, God! I can't say it enough. My heart is filled to the brim with gratitude for the wonderful miracles you have brought into my life. Every day I find something to be grateful for, in the smile of a child, the laughter of a good friend, or the warmth of the sun as I walk outside. The world is abundant with reasons why I should thank you each and every day, and I know that even greater abundance will be mine. Thank you, God.

For once you were in darkness, but now in the Lord you are light. Live as children of light—for the fruit of the light is found in all that is good and right and true.
—Ephesians 5:8–9

Lord, how easy it is to express gratitude when times are good, but how difficult it can be for us to also thank you for the hard times— especially when we are in the midst of them. That's not wise, Lord, and we are sorry. For when we look back over all the ups and downs

of our lives, we see that you were in fact working all things together for good. For lessons
learned in the hard times and for the strength
you gave us to get through them, we give you
thanks. After all, how can we not be grateful
for something that brings us closer to you? So
thank you, Lord, for the hard times.

Heavenly God, I thank you that even in the
depths of my deepest pain, I can still feel your
presence and love. Even when all seems bleak
and dark, through your holy words, I know
that I am never really alone. Because of your
Son, Jesus Christ, I am protected for all eter-
nity. This assurance allows me hope, and I am
so thankful that I am saved by your mercy and
redeemed by your love. Amen.

For God so loved the world that he gave his only Son, so that everyone who believes in him may not perish but may have eternal life.
—John 3:16

Father God, how glad I am that you put so many precious friends in my life over the years. When I look back through time I can still see their faces and remember their encouragement and love, even if time and distance have separated us. Never let me take my friends for granted, Lord. I praise and thank you for the ones I've known and the ones I've yet to meet! Friendship is one of your greatest gifts, and I'm so glad you thought of it.

A friend loves at all times.
—Proverbs 17:17

God, I admit that there are many times in my day that I forget to focus on what I have. I am so consumed with what I want and need that I often lose track of the amazing and abundant blessings you have already given me. Please help me shift my focus back to the good things that surround me, no matter how simple they might be. Too often I find myself worrying about my life, wanting to do more and achieve more and have more, and then I am without peace. Guide me back to that place within where I am aware of all the treasures you have placed before me. Amen.

Father in Heaven, you have made it so easy for us. You have let us know exactly what is expected of us. We don't have to guess at your will, for you have set it out plainly in black and white for us to follow. Your rules are not capricious or random, but specific and simple. Thank you for telling us your desires for us so plainly and for forgiving us our shortcomings when we fail. Your mercy and love give us hope that someday we can live in accordance with your law. Amen.

One of the scribes came near and heard them disputing with one another, and seeing that he answered them well, he asked him, "Which commandment is the first of all?" Jesus answered, "The first is, 'Hear, O Israel: the Lord our God, the Lord is one; you shall love the Lord your God with all your heart, and with all your soul, and with all your mind, and with all your strength.' The second is this, 'You shall love your neighbor as yourself.' There is no other commandment greater than these."

—Mark 12:28–31

Lord, I sometimes feel I am not worthy of all the good you have given me. But I know that you love all your children equally, and I am honored to be the recipient of your bountiful blessings. I look around me each day and am in awe of how much you have given me, not just in material things, but also the people you have chosen to enter my life. I am grateful for the lessons I've learned, even though many of them were learned the hard way. Thank you for continuing to bless me with even more good things, and I promise to choose to do all I can to be worthy of them. Amen.

God, I sometimes forget to thank you for the things you have given me. I rush about my days and nights, distracted by the busyness, and forget to stop and look around at all the miracles you have brought into my life. Thank you. I mean that from the bottom of my heart. Thank you. I am overwhelmed by the mercy you have shown me when I screwed up, the grace you have given me when I most needed it, and the love you never cease to give, even when I don't act like I deserve it. Thank you, God. Thank you so much.

For he delivers the needy when they call,
the poor and those who have no helper.
He has pity on the weak and the needy,
and saves the lives of the needy.
—Psalm 72:12–13

Teach me, Lord, to look at the world with hope and expectation, not with despair and lack. I am grateful for all you have done for me, but there is still this emptiness inside that catches up to me now and then. Help me see how wonderful my life is, just as it is, and that nothing more is needed to be happy and at peace,

Prayers of Gratitude

for those are gifts that come from within.
Teach me to keep my eyes on the bounty that
comes from a thankful heart, not from the
things we acquire but from the experiences we
have and the love we give. Amen.

Dear Father, today I just couldn't seem to see
the good in my life. I know it is there, and
believe me, I am thankful for it, but when I am
mired in the daily issues of family and home
and work, it is hard to shift my focus. Please be
gentle with me, and be patient as I work harder
to shift my focus onto the blessings and away
from the problems. I know in my heart that
once I accomplish this more good things will
come into my life, reminding me always of your
loving and prosperous spirit. Amen.

Now thank we all our God
with hearts and hands and voices,
who wondrous things hath done,
in whom his world rejoices;
who, from our mothers' arms,
hath blessed us on our way
with countless gifts of love,
and still is ours today.
—Martin Rinkart, translated by Catherine Winkworth,
"Now Thank We All Our God"

Dear God, the ability to talk to you directly and bring my cares and needs to you is nothing short of incredible. That a being of your magnitude and limitless power wants to have a personal relationship with each of your creatures amazes me! Thank you for giving us the opportunity to feel your presence daily. Knowing you are near me makes me love you more. Amen.

Lord, how difficult it is for us to pray, believing that you hear us, but how necessary it is to do so—to express our gratitude in advance for all the answers you are preparing to lavish upon us as we pray. Help my unbelief, Lord. When I come to you in prayer, may I do so believing that you always have my best interests at heart. Whether your answer is yes, no, or not now, you do hear me! And so, Lord, I thank you now even before I see evidence of your work in my life.

And this is the boldness we have in him,
that if we ask anything according to his will,
he hears us.
—1 John 5:14

Lord, would you think it insincere if I said thanks for the wrinkles and gray hair? What if

I said thanks for the extra padding around my hips or for the creaking in my knees when I climb the stairs? You see, I've come to understand that growing older is not a right, it's a privilege not everyone is granted. And should you give me the opportunity to grow gracefully into a contented old person, with an abundance of grandchildren and great-grandchildren, I will be blessed beyond belief! And so I choose to replace my grumbling about aging with gratitude for the gift. Thank you, Lord.

Gray hair is a crown of glory;
it is gained in a righteous life.
—Proverbs 16:31